This book is presented
by
First Lady Christie Vilsack
on behalf of
Iowa Stories 2000

This book belongs to:

Best wishes to
the children
of Wilton —
Lois
Ericksson

Thank You to Our Sponsors

THE LEADER IN THE FIELD

Innova Ideas & Services
Sigler Printing & Publishing
McMillen Publishing
United Fulfillment Solutions

District 6000 Rotary

IOWA SOYBEAN PROMOTION BOARD

CASEY'S GENERAL STORES, INC.

Day-Lee Foods, Inc.

First Data

KIKKOMAN FOODS FOUNDATION, INC.

Nippon Life Insurance Company of America

NSK Corporation

Toyota Financial Services

Iowa Sister States
Humanities Iowa
Iowa Arts Council
State Library of Iowa
Iowa Department of Education

Foreword

Sweet Corn and Sushi is a true story about the friendship between the people of the state of Iowa and the people of the prefecture of Yamanashi, Japan. Iowa writer Lori Erickson tells how Iowans airlifted hogs to Yamanashi after a typhoon destroyed the hog population there in 1959. The Yamanashi government sent money to Iowa when we suffered through the floods of 1993. Will Thomson's watercolor pictures help illustrate the customs of each country—some similar, some very different.

In 1999 Lori and I traveled to Japan where we visited schools, libraries, and museums. We talked with women about concerns that we share, especially those that affect our children and grandchildren. We wanted to find a way to celebrate this special friendship between Iowa and Yamanashi and encourage children to learn more about our friends and neighbors around the world. Did you know that the people of Yamanashi celebrate "Iowa Day" every year? They hold a potluck supper, display Iowa quilts, and share stories. I even milked a cow and learned to eat with chopsticks.

My foundation, Iowa Stories 2000, is giving a copy of this book to every kindergartner and kindergarten teacher in Iowa. You will notice that the book is translated into Japanese, because we plan to give a copy to every elementary school library and every public library in Yamanashi, Japan.

I hope you and your families will read *Sweet Corn and Sushi* together. Maybe you can check some other books out of your library about Japan and other countries you'd like to visit some day. Maybe you can check the Internet for more information about Yamanashi. We have learned from research that it is very important for children to read non-fiction books as well as fiction.

With the book is a map of Iowa and Yamanashi that you can color. On the back are directions for origami, the art of paper folding, which Lori and I learned when we visited Japan.

Many people, companies and organizations helped make it possible for Tom and me to give this book to 41,000 children and teachers. You will see our sponsors listed in the front of this book. I'd like to extend a special thanks to Iowa's Area Education Agencies, Iowa Telecom and Grinnell Verizon employees and their friends and families for assembling and distributing the books and related materials.

Christie Vilsack
First Lady of Iowa

Please read to a child.
It may be the best part of your day.

Sweet Corn and Sushi

THE STORY OF IOWA AND YAMANASHI

Written by Lori Erickson
Illustrated by Will Thomson
Japanese Translation by Yasuo Ohdera & Shinji Yoda

Published by Lori Erickson

Layout/Design and Printing by:

413 Northwestern Avenue
Ames, IA 50010
515-232-0208

www.mcmillenbooks.com

Designed by Dave Popelka & Will Thomson

Library of Congress Control Number: 2004102802

ISBN: 1-888223-55-3

Dedication

This book is dedicated to the children of Iowa and
Yamanashi, and especially to Owen and Carl.

Acknowledgements

The author and illustrator gratefully
acknowledge the invaluable assistance of Iowa
First Lady Christie Vilsack, Cyndi Pederson,
Yasuo Ohdera, Shinji Yoda, Jean Lloyd-Jones,
Yuko Oshima, and Yuko Tanaka.

遠くはなれた、たくさんの違いのある、二つの美しい土地それぞれに、誇り高い人々が住んでいました。

これは、その人たちの間にめばえ、大きく花開いた、すばらしい友情の物語です。

Once there were two beautiful lands and two proud peoples separated by great distance and many differences. This is the story of how a wonderful friendship has blossomed between them.

1

One land is Yamanashi, a prefecture on the main island of Honshu in Japan. In Yamanashi steep mountains covered with tall trees tower above valleys dense with cities and towns.

その土地の一つは山梨県。日本の本州にあります。山梨では森におおわれた
けわしい山々が、盆地に広がる都市や町を囲むようにそびえています。

もう一つはアイオワ州。アメリカ中西部にあります。アイオワでは、ゆるやかに波打つ緑の丘が、地平線までつづいています。豊かな土地に、パッチワークのようにひろがる畑の合間に、小さな町や都市が散りばめられています。

The other land is Iowa, a state in the middle of the United States. Here green hills stretch like waves to the horizon, and small towns and cities lie sprinkled across a patchwork landscape of rich fields.

Like many stories, the tale of Iowa and Yamanashi begins in conflict. From 1941 to 1945, Japan and the United States fought against each other in World War II. Many thousands of people were killed, and grieving families in both nations mourned their lost loved ones. It was a time of great hardship and sadness.

After the war ended people in Japan and America slowly rebuilt their lives, but often feelings of bitterness remained.

ほかのいくつかの物語のように、この山梨とアイオワのお話も、争いごとからはじまりました。1941年から1945年までつづいた第二次世界大戦で、日本とアメリカは、おたがいに敵として戦いました。両方の国で、何万人もの人々が殺され、愛する家族を失った人々は、深い悲しみに沈んでいました。それは、大きな苦しみと悲しみの時代でした。

戦いが終った後、人々はそれぞれの生活をだんだんと立て直しましたが、悲しい思い出は、いつまでも残りました。

それから十数年たった１９５９年、山梨の人々にもう一つ別の大きな苦しみがもたらされました。大きな台風が、一ヶ月に二度もつづけて山梨県をおそい、激しい風とふりつづく雨が、人々を苦しめたのです。やっと嵐が去った後に残されたのは、荒れはてた土地だけでした。

In 1959, the people of Yamanashi suffered another blow when two terrible typhoons pounded the region within less than a month, bringing relentless rain and fierce winds. When the last storm finally ended, much of Yamanashi lay destroyed.

Richard Thomas, an Iowan who had served with the U.S. military in Japan, heard of the devastation and wanted to do something to help. He told other Iowans about what had happened and asked what could be done.

When the people of Iowa heard about the great disaster half a world away, they didn't think of how they had once been at war with Japan, or of how their sons, brothers, and fathers had once fought the people of Yamanashi. Instead the Iowans saw only that these people were suffering and that they needed help.

戦後、日本でアメリカ軍の仕事をしていたことのあるアイオワの人、リチャード・トーマスは、その大災害のことを聞いた時、なんとか山梨の人々を助けてあげたいと思いました。彼は、アイオワの人々に、何が起きたのかを伝え、何かできることはないだろうかと相談しました。

アイオワの人々は、地球の裏側の大災害のことを聞いたとき、日本との戦争のこと、そして、自分たちの親や兄弟あるいは息子たちが、かつて山梨の人々と戦ったことは考えませんでした。ただ、山梨の人々が今とても困っているということ、そして助けが必要である、ということだけを考えました。

6

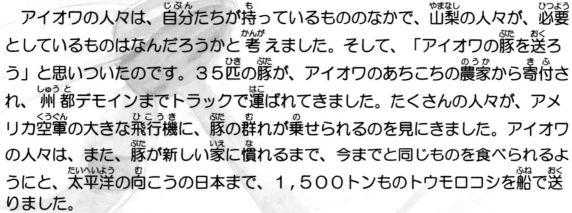

アイオワの人々は、自分たちが持っているもののなかで、山梨の人々が、必要としているものはなんだろうかと考えました。そして、「アイオワの豚を送ろう」と思いついたのです。３５匹の豚が、アイオワのあちこちの農家から寄付され、州都デモインまでトラックで運ばれてきました。たくさんの人々が、アメリカ空軍の大きな飛行機に、豚の群れが乗せられるのを見にきました。アイオワの人々は、また、豚が新しい家に慣れるまで、今までと同じものを食べられるようにと、太平洋の向こうの日本まで、１，５００トンものトウモロコシを船で送りました。

The Iowans thought of what they had that Yamanashi needed, and came up with the idea for an "Iowa Hog Lift." Farmers from around the state donated 35 hogs and sent them by truck to the state capital of Des Moines. Many people came to see them herded on board a big U.S. Air Force plane. The people of Iowa also sent 1,500 tons of corn by ship across the ocean, so the pigs would have familiar food while they got used to their new home.

From Des Moines it took three days to fly to Japan, because air-planes didn't travel as fast in those days. The plane made stops in California, Hawaii, and Wake Island in the middle of the Pacific Ocean, giving these hogs a look at more of the world than probably any pigs in Iowa's history.

そのころの飛行機は、今のように速くはなかったので、デモインから日本まで３日かかりました。飛行機は、カリフォルニア、ハワイ、そして、太平洋の真ん中にあるウェイク島に立ち寄りました。その間、きっと、この３５匹の豚は、アイオワの歴史の中で、ほかのどの豚よりも、世界のより多くのものを見ることができたことでしょう。

Imagine how surprised they must have been when they arrived in Yamanashi! Instead of rolling fields of corn and soybeans they saw tall mountains. All the people gathered to meet them at the airport spoke a different language than what they were used to hearing. And when they got off the plane they were offered a snack of Japanese radishes and carrots, for them an unusual— but very tasty— treat.

山梨に着いた時、この３５匹の豚がどれほどおどろいたか、想像してみてください。トウモロコシと大豆の畑がつづく波うつ丘のかわりに、高い山々を見たのです。空港に集まってきた人たちは、今まで聞いたことのない言葉を話していたのです。飛行機からおりた時、３５匹の豚は、日本のにんじんと大根を食べさせてもらいました。不思議な、でも、とてもおいしいごちそうでした。

In Yamanashi, people were amazed that strangers from across the world were sending them a gift. While the hogs helped restore their livestock industry, even more important was the love and hope for the future they represented.

山梨の人々は、地球の反対側に住む、まったく知らない人々からの贈物におどろきました。送られた豚は、山梨の畜産業の立て直しに役立ちました。そして、もっと大事なこととして、未来への希望と愛のきっかけともなったのです。

台風の被害から立ち直った後も、山梨の人々は、自分たちを助けてくれたアイオワの人々の親切を、けっして忘れませんでした。そして、離れたところに住む人々が、おたがいに強く結びつき、特別な友情をはぐくんでいけるようにと、山梨県とアイオワ州が姉妹県になることを提案しました。1960年、二つの地域は、アメリカと日本のあいだで最初の姉妹県となりました。その一年後、山梨県は、新しい友情のしるしとして、特別な贈り物～大きな青銅の鐘と鐘楼～を贈りました。それには、アイオワの人々へのお礼の気持ちがこめられていました。

Even after Yamanashi recovered from the typhoons, its people did not forget the generosity of the Iowans who had helped them. They invited Iowa to be their sister state, meaning that the two regions would have a special friendship binding them together. In 1960, the relationship became the first sister-state bond between the United States and Japan. A year later Yamanashi sent a very special present to Iowa to mark the new friendship: a huge bronze temple bell and bell house, a gift of gratitude from the people of Yamanashi to the people of Iowa.

Through the decades since then, the friendship between the two states has grown ever deeper.

Hundreds of people have traveled back and forth between Iowa and Yamanashi, including teachers, farmers, artists, business people, and school children. Staying in people's homes, they have gotten the chance to see what life in America and Japan is really like.

People from Yamanashi have ridden in RAGBRAI, the week-long bicycle ride across Iowa held each July. They've eaten corn on the cob and homemade apple pie, have milked cows and visited the Iowa State Fair.

それから数十年のあいだに、アイオワ州と山梨県の友情は、さらに深まっていきました。多くの人々が、それぞれの間を行き来しました。学校の先生、農家の人々、芸術家や実業家、そして学生や生徒たち。おたがいの家々に滞在し、アメリカと日本の生活が、本当はどのようなものか体験することができました。

山梨の人々は、毎年7月に一週間かけて行われる、アイオワ横断自転車ツアー、ラグブライに参加しました。もぎたてのトウモロコシや、手作りのアップルパイを食べ、牛の乳をしぼり、年に一度の有名な博覧会、アイオワステイトフェアを見に行きました。

一方、アイオワの人々は、山梨を訪れ、富士山に登り、深い地下からわき出る温泉につかり、もぎたてのブドウを食べました。帰りには、たくさんの思い出と写真、そしてあたらしく芽生えた友情を、お土産に持って帰りました。

People from Iowa have come to Yamanashi to climb the sacred mountain of Mt. Fuji, have soaked in hot springs bubbling up from deep under the earth, and have eaten grapes just picked from the vine. When they return home, they bring memories, photos, and new friendships.

13

And in 1993, when the people of Iowa suffered from a devastating flood that drove people from their homes and destroyed many crops, the people of Yamanashi sent hundreds of thousands of dollars to help those who were suffering. Even after 34 years, they had not forgotten the help Iowans had sent them after the typhoons of 1959.

１９９３年、今度は、アイオワの人々が、大洪水に苦しめられました。多くの人が家を失い、農作物に大きな被害がでました。その時、山梨の人々は、たくさんのお見舞い金を、被害にあった人々のために送りました。３４年前、１９５９年に台風に苦しめられた時、アイオワの人々から受けた親切を、忘れてはいなかったのです。

今でも、この二つの美しい土地、山梨とアイオワには、たくさんの違いがあります。
　山梨では、ごはん、うどんやそば、すしなどを、はしで食べます。アイオワでは、牛肉や豚肉やポテト料理などを、ナイフ、フォーク、スプーンで食べます。ゆでたトウモロコシは、子どもたちの大好物です。

Today there are many differences between these two beautiful lands. Children in Yamanashi use chopsticks to eat rice, noodles, and sushi, a delicacy made with raw fish. In Iowa, a meal is often potatoes served with beef or pork, eaten with a spoon, fork, and knife. Sweet corn is a favorite of many Iowa children.

If you are a child in Yamanashi, you take off your shoes before entering your house and school. In Iowa, your parents may want you to take off your muddy shoes but often you forget!

山梨では、家や学校の中に入る前に、くつをぬぎます。アイオワでは、家の中でもくつをはいているのが一般的です。そのため、お父さんやお母さんが、くつがどろで汚れた時は、それをぬいで入るように言っても、子どもたちは、ついつい忘れてしまいがちです。

山梨の子どもたちは、長くて色とりどりのこいのぼりが見られる "こどもの日" や、家族とごちそうを食べ、お年玉がもらえる "お正月" が大好きです。
また、アイオワの子どもたちは、いろいろな仮装をして家々をまわり、袋いっぱいにキャンディーを集める "ハロウィン" や、パレードや花火で祝う7月4日の "独立記念日" を楽しみにしています。

Children in Yamanashi love *Kodomo-no-Hi* or Children's Day, when homes where girls and boys live are decorated with long, colorful streamers, and *O-Shogatsu*, a celebration of the New Year, when families have parties and children get little envelopes with money inside from their relatives. In Iowa, kids look forward to Halloween, when they dress up in costumes and collect bags full of candy, and the Fourth of July, when people celebrate America's independence with parades and fireworks.

17

In Yamanashi, ancient traditions are cherished. Centuries-old temples and shrines draw people to celebrate Buddhist and Shinto rituals. Graceful arts like calligraphy, flower arranging, and the tea ceremony remind people of Japan's long and proud history. On special occasions, women dress in brilliantly colored kimonos, the traditional robes of old Japan.

山梨の人々は、古くからの伝統を大切にしてきました。何百年も前に建てられたお寺や神社にお参りし、書道、生け花、茶道などの美しい伝統芸術に親しみ、日本の長い歴史を大切にしています。特別な日には、女の人たちが古くからの伝統衣装である、はなやかな着物を着ます。

アイオワでは農村の伝統が生活を形づくってきました。今では、多くの人々が、都市や町に住んでいますが、大地の美しさと恵みから、遠く離れてしまったわけではありません。豊かな農地が都市や町を囲み、種まき、栽培、そして、刈り入れなどが、季節の移りかわりとともにおこなわれます。ビーズ細工やキルティングのような芸術は、かつてアイオワに住んでいた原住民や開拓者たちから引き継がれたもので、その後、移り住んできた人々も、それぞれの音楽や物語、文化をアイオワにもたらしました。

In Iowa, rural traditions have shaped much of life. Though many Iowans now live in towns and cities, the bounty and beauty of the land are never far away. Fertile farms surround every city and town, and the cycles of planting, cultivating, and harvest mark the passing seasons. Arts like beadwork and quilting remind people of the state's Native American and pioneer pasts, and more recent immigrants have brought their own songs, stories, and cultures to the state.

Iowa and Yamanashi also have much in common. While the two states have many modern, high-tech industries, agriculture is very important to both. In Iowa the main crops are corn, soybeans, and hogs, while Yamanashi is famous for its delicious grapes, peaches, and other fruits.

アイオワと山梨には、たくさんの 共通点 もあります。現代的なハイテク 産業 が盛んになった今も、農業はどちらにとっても 重要な産業です。アイオワで は、トウモロコシや大豆の栽培、そして豚の飼育が盛んです。一方、山梨は、ぶ どうや桃など、果物の産地として有名です。

どちらの土地でも、四季の変化は、人々に自然のリズムを感じさせます。春、山梨では桜の花が咲き、アイオワでは、チューリップとラッパスイセンが咲きます。ともに、むしあつい夏の後には、紅葉で色づいたさわやかな秋が続きます。冬が訪れると、山梨では、雪が白い毛布のように山々をおおい、寒さが厳しいアイオワでは、激しい吹雪が吹き荒れ、雪が深く積もります。

In both lands, four seasons keep people in touch with the rhythms of nature. In Yamanashi, spring brings cherry blossoms; in Iowa, tulips and daffodils. Both lands have hot and humid summers followed by crisp autumns with blazing leaves. Winter is harsher in Iowa, with fierce blizzards that bring many inches of snow, but snow also falls on Yamanashi, laying a soft blanket of white on mountainsides.

Children in both lands love books, television, and video games. In Iowa, more and more children are learning Japanese martial arts like karate, while in Yamanashi, many people love baseball.

どちらの子どもたちも、本やテレビ、そしてビデオゲームが大好きです。アイオワでは、空手などの日本の武道を、習う子どもが増えてきました。山梨では、たくさんの子どもたちが野球を楽しんでいます。

どちらの子どもたちも、夜、お父さんやお母さんに、ふとんを掛けてもらいながら、「グッド　ナイト」または「おやすみなさい」とささやいてもらい、眠りにつきます。

And in both lands, children are tucked into bed each night by their parents, who whisper "good night" or *"oyasuminasai"* in their ears as they fall asleep.

Many years after the terrible typhoons, the ties between Yamanashi and Iowa have become like a silken ribbon. Each slender strand of silk is so fine and delicate that it can be broken with a finger, but when it is put together with other strands, it forms a band as strong as it is lovely.

恐ろしい台風から長い時がたった今、アイオワと山梨のきずなは、絹でできたリボンにたとえることができます。絹の糸の一本一本は、細くて弱くて、指でも簡単に切れてしまえるぐらいのものです。それが何本も集まり、重なり合ったとき、強くて美しいリボンになります。

In 1959 a single silken strand joined the two lands: the loving concern of a single man. Today the two lands are linked by a beautifully varied ribbon of friendship that unites the children, grandchildren, and great-grandchildren of the people who were once at war.

１９５９年、一本の絹の糸が、二つの土地を結びつけました。それは、一人の男の人の思いやりでした。今日、様々な美しい友情で織り上げられたリボンが、山梨とアイオワを、強く結びつけています。かつては戦争で戦ったことのある人々の手から、その子ども、孫、ひ孫たちへと受けつがれながら・・・。

If you are a child in Iowa, someday when you are older you can travel to Yamanashi to see rice paddies growing beneath tall mountains. You can watch the sunrise from the top of Mt. Fuji and marvel at ancient temples and serene gardens.

Over plates of sushi you can learn more about Japan and tell your new friends about life in Iowa.

もし、あなたがアイオワの子どもだったら、大きくなったとき、いつか山梨を訪れることがあるかもしれません。その時は、高い山々のふもとで、豊に育つ稲を見るかもしれません。また、富士山の頂上から太陽が昇るのを見たり、古いお寺や神社のすばらしさ、その庭の静けさに、おどろいたりするかもしれません。あたらしい友だちとおすしを食べながら、日本についてもっと学び、その友だちには、アイオワのくらしについて話しているかもしれません。

26

もし、あなたが山梨の子どもだったら、いつかアイオワを訪ねて、花でいっぱいの大草原を見て、夏の雷と嵐のすごさにおどろくかもしれません。そして、ミシシッピ川を船でくだり、もぎたての甘くておいしいトウモロコシを食べているかもしれません。

And if you are a child in Yamanashi, someday you can travel to Iowa, where you can see prairie flowers carpeting hillsides and thrill to thunderstorms blowing across a wide summer sky. You can ride a riverboat down the Mississippi River, and eat freshly picked sweet corn.

Whether you live in Iowa or Yamanashi, know that there
are many friends waiting for you half a world away.

今、あなたがアイオワに住んでいたとしても、山梨に住んでいたとしても、
地球の反対側でたくさんのお友だちが、あなたを待っているということを忘れな
いでください・・・。